Let Out the Djinn
Jane Aldous

ARACHNE PRESS

First published in UK 2019 by Arachne Press Limited
100 Grierson Road, London SE23 1NX
www.arachnepress.com
© Jane Aldous 2019
ISBN: 978-1-909208-81-0
The moral rights of the author have been asserted.

Thanks to Muireann Grealy for her proofing.
Printed on wood-free paper in the UK by TJ International, Padstow.

Acknowledgements

Andromeda on All Hallows' Eve (2014), *A Dead Lamb in Polbain* (2015) and *Whale Wall* (2012) were published in Northwords Now.

As a Song Thrush Sings was commended in the Buzzwords Poetry Competition 2016.

Black Wing Rock was published on line on the Stanza Poetry Map of Scotland.

Eel Ghazal won the Wigtown Poetry Competition and was published in Southlight, both in 2012.

Goodbye Voyager 1 was commended in the Baker Prize 2013.

Lochinver Harbour was highly commended in the Norman MacCaig Centenary Competition 2010.

The Shoe Doll and *Washerwomen on Calton Hill* were performed in the City Arts Centre and published by Edinburgh Museums and Galleries, for the year of History, Heritage and Archaeology in 2017.

Washerwomen on Calton Hill was also published by New Writing Scotland 2017.

A version of *With Meme on Mellon Udrigle Beach* was longlisted for the Bridport Poetry Prize 2012.

I would also like to acknowledge all the amazing support for my poetry from my lovely partner Bev.

Also, all the friendship and encouragement from my original poetry group, Lindy Barbour, Anthony Costello, Alex Devoy, Anita John, Simon MacLaren, Sheila Wild and more recently Pat McCaw.

Finally, my brilliant editor Cherry Potts who had faith in me.

Jane Aldous is an Edinburgh-based poet. Some of Jane's poems have been published in literary magazines such as *Northwords Now* and *Southlight*. She's been commended in poetry competitions and she won the Wigtown Prize in 2012. Her poems have also been anthologised.

Arachne Press has previously published her poems in the following anthologies

Dusk 2018

An Outbreak of Peace 2018

Noon 2019

Contents

Let Out the Djinn

For Bev

Telegram from Doris Court Nursing Home

Greetings!
Here she is your chick, your slick of blood, skin, bone.
Here they are, your ma and pa, they're terrified,
she's sore, he thinks he's going to drop you.
Congratulations.
Love, Min and Avis.
Stop.

Let out the Djinn

At four she had a snapshot thought,
she was a spinning top
whirling in the vastness of a wide, dark world.

Familiars started visiting, invisible friends,
characters stepping out of books, voices within,
leading her out into swirling haar.

She kissed a girl next door, listened to tales
in the woods by the shore, sat in her bedroom
writing poems and stories.

Sometimes she woke in the night, slippery creatures
on her chest, sometimes she danced with dervish
disco dancers on claggy floors.

But all her daemons slunk away into cobweb
corners, no-one listened anymore. Then
after her mother died, a barn owl flew

and, flinging open all the doors and windows,
out they came, laughing, tumbling about, grinning
like little skulls of garlic bulbs, bumblebees in her brain,

words skittering in the birch tree breeze, the Djinn,
all her familiars, friends, she'd let them out again,
summoned them, returned to herself.

Portland Road

The cat was lost for a week after we moved
to live next door to the Bastow brothers
and their mother on Portland Road.

They kept a tidy workshop, cold chisels clean
as missiles, nails in boxes, saws and drills hooked
on beams. Their vests and long-johns hung in the yard.

One brother never left Babbacombe, the other had
been as far as Torquay. Their mother gave us a wooden-
handled Victorian umbrella to shield us from the sun.

But the stack of girls' magazines, neatly tied with string
and left by our back door, was the thing that clung
awkwardly between us. They were deemed unsuitable
so ended up as underlay for the Wilton carpet.

How it was

Parcelled up in waistcoat and gun belt,
I killed every adult at point blank range.

I wandered out in sea-fog and kissed
a girl in a concrete shelter.

I searched the Bible and dictionaries
for someone like me.

With acne raging I bought chocolates
for the groundkeeper's daughter.

I wrote to Woman's Own.
Miss Crocker, the Chemistry teacher

played cricket for England, wore black leathers
and rode a 1500cc but for a while,

my heart belonged to Mrs Dunball
our English teacher.

I wondered if Miss Crocker and Miss Mulvaney
lived together and if they did, did anyone mind?

One day I told the groundkeeper's daughter
I loved her and she said don't be silly.

After that I kissed girls in draughty flats, cars,
and on sticky dance floors.

I read The Well of Loneliness as a rite of passage.
I had words for who I was and didn't like them.

I didn't like the poisonous letter, being sent
for a healing, or reading Miss A loves Miss D

chalked on the blackboard, or my mother shouting
It's all about bed isn't it! or Clause 28.

I never wanted a name to describe myself,
never wanted to feel: less than, unentitled.

And now looking back, my ghosts seem like
standing stones, silent crows,

they've done their worst, they're only stories
now.

Finding Bluebells

An urban ingénue and a denim dude,
we stood apart from the Half Moon Lane
crowd. I was drawn in by your open-necked
shirt and olive skin.

Next date, down at the Gates, I was timid
but thought who cares if some women
have painted moustaches and look like men.
You were untouchable but when you put
your hand down my shirt, I was gone.

Living your life indoors, on your bed,
in your head, I remember you rented
a room from your mother who lived
in a Shepherd's Bush basement.

Until then I'd never seen squares of
newsprint hanging on string beside a toilet,
eaten curry or heard Van Morrison.

You said: come and meet my brother
up the stairs. Someone handed me
a joint and through the fug you told me you'd
never left London, never seen bluebells.

I drove us out until we found a bluebell
wood and stayed on for a pub. Later you called
to say your brother had overdosed and died.

It was all over for us,
we argued about drugs.
So much for love, I thought.

Dave Off in Five

Your diary says, the 17 May 1944 was
a lovely sunny day. Then at 9.55 am, a day
out of Naples, your ship *Dempo* was torpedoed,
starboard side aft, fifty miles from Bourgie.
You spotted that deadly chevron nosing straight
for the hull, ran back for your greatcoat before
jumping into a lifeboat.
Dave off in five, your entries sound as if
you're writing about someone else.
Did the whole thing only take five minutes?
Two hours later you were all rescued by *Catterick's*
crew, but watched another convoy ship go down.
The retrieval of your coat became a story repeated
down the years. Still makes me wonder, how your life
would have been if there had been no war,
where your dreams would have taken you?

In the New Leaf Co-op

All sorts of souls come here, the ones
who rush, the ones with bikes and others
like yesterday's, who wandered in all smiles,
with empty bottles in her rucksack.
I could have done the refills in no time
but I know fine what these old girls are like.
Thank goodness we weren't busy, it only takes
one dizzy person to clear the shop.

Instead I watched from the counter as she bent down,
held on to the shelf, stood up, went white, dithered,
whispering something to herself.
Finally she arrived at the till and I smiled back thinking,
I wonder if I'll get like that, cobweb hair poking from
under a cock-eyed hat, old eyes like vintage glass.

Crow's Eye

Moving slowly from cage to cage,
she was observed by a hobbled crow,
its head to one side, a makeshift leg
scraping the floor. She'd promised
that the bird would be the last of them,
her patients, the blinded owls, one-legged
magpies, wounded wood pigeons.
She'd lived so long like this she couldn't
think how else it might be. The crow
pecked grain between the floorboards;
its eye seemed like a window on another
world, a blank page, Antarctica.
She shook out her bones like a hen
in a dust bath. One day she'd surprise
them all, pack the car, find somewhere
else, as long as she had her birds, could
look a crow in the eye, see where it took them.

Watching the Celts on Leith Walk

He squeezes his eyes shut, opens them up,
tries to focus through dank, grey air
between tenements and traffic.
Torcs are jewelling the necks of warriors,
on their way to battle, they're strung out,
exhausted, their garments bloodied,
he can half see them, half not.
With an un-gloved hand he reaches out,
touches the rim of a rubbish bin,
steadies himself, perches in the bus shelter
like a migratory bird.
Fingering thin grey tufts, spun across
his bare scalp, he becomes an ethereal shape,
one of the lava faces, shapeless, graceless,
in a shuffle of bodies unseen on the crossing
who might have gone under the wheels,
if he'd been less alive, staring at a screen
like one of those sharp-suited young things,
he thought, if only he'd kept those wings.

With Meme on Mellon Udrigle Beach

Come away Meme put your swimsuit on,
sink your feet in the hot shell sand. You can

paddle or swim in the turquoise sea and put
your robe on afterwards. Does this remind

you of Borth or Newquay when you were
holding the camera and I was running?

In every place you made a home, even in the
early stages of dementia you varnished floors

and put up curtains. But after that last night when
you were wrapped in a blanket on the stairs

you never returned, instead it was daily Risperidone
and a basement room. So come away,

we can walk past the white cottages, watch swallows
flying low over the sheep fields and stay as long as you like.

Death Waiting

He sat neat, bearded, slightly harassed
across the desk from young parents
whose arms were full of squirming children,
as I knocked on the door of the Registrar's Office.
Would you like to wait or return in half an hour?
he said. So I found myself in a room across the corridor
used for everything and nothing in particular.
It could have been an hour or day later
when the Registrar's door re-opened
and I overheard him speaking on the phone,
I'll have to go now, I think I've got a death waiting.

Malmesbury

Stay where you are tight in the earth,
it's not for you to worry anymore.
I'm the one still turning over memories
encased in their globes,
shaking them up, tapping the glass,
making no impression on the past.
I want to know where all the energy of life ends up.
Is it in breath wafting from parent to child
as it did from the off or as it does even now,
when I hear the football scores or notice a flower?
That's when I get snagged, imagining that in a pocket of air,
down some street, if I cared to look you'd still be there.
Death's final twist is not the sense of ending
it's breath on glass and little acts of remembering.

Home Service

Perhaps the best song is sung by a robin
from a birch tree one morning, unrehearsed,
the best beach, the one with the whitest shell sand,
the sweetest kiss, our first on the beach at Aberlady,
my favourite time, a time without end, half listening
to the radio, half writing that poem which somehow
will never get written…

Whisper

No one but him knew how a dog could feel,
falling to earth.

How cool the meadow would be,
after the harness was unhooked.

Nothing's going to happen to her, he'd say,
Whisper's connected with twenty thousand
pounds of straps, we're good.

Every time we went climbing,
I'd be tucked inside his jacket.

We'd be on top of a ridge and he'd talk to me
like no-one else did.

Then we'd jump and we'd fly, down, down
and I'd be wearing goggles and a head band.

That last time, he left without me.
Bet he's still flying,

bet he is.

Whisper belonged to Dean Potter who took her BASE jumping.

Lochinver Harbour

Fortitude and *Spinningdale*,
Dorothy Ann and *Bressay Bank*
from Ullapool, Fraserborough,
Fleetwood and Boulogne.
Four trawlers roped up alongside
four hundred ghost ships.

Silver sea washes up
the concrete harbour walls.
On the quayside shadows flit
through empty fish-selling sheds
where crushed ice has spilled
around fish boxes, creels and ropes.

As *Fortitude* stands dry docked,
its freshly painted lacquer
merging with the reek of fish,
Spinningdale's crew stack boxes,
shouting to be heard over
the churning engine and spitting bilges.

But the old skiffs, trawlers, luggers
and herring boats once hauling in
all the silver darlings have long gone,
the fish-gutters, curers and fishwives too.
For them, for us, the shimmering shoals
no longer run.

Whale Wall

As he scraped remnants of flesh
from the carcass of the dead pilot whale,
Trevor spoke of whale sightings
and death accumulations of fossils.

Once he had seen an Orca pod
steal up on a RIB full of Antarctic tourists,
as he'd gripped the tiller and stared hard
into the eye of a killer whale.

A man whose arthritic hands now pulled
wires tight through the bleached skeleton,
fixing it to the whitewashed bothy wall:
a whale leaping into its own shadow.

A whale skeleton fixed to Bothy wall, Kilchoan, Ardnamurchan, NW Highlands.

Eel Ghazal

A brown eel caught itself on a casually thrown hook,
Anguilla anguilla where are all the marshland glass wrigglers?

Weir and dam, net trap and poison you slithery boy
as tricky as a spiv closing in on the next deal.

Brown fen lurker, yellow canal threader, green mud swimmer,
an elusive thought slipping in and out like a rumour.

Surreptitiously you respond to an ancient voice,
the Sargasso pulling you back into its mysterious stillness.

Only your offspring return, catching the current –
eel breed, eel feed for your lives, for all of your long dark
lives.

Highland Ghazal

Let's take the path to Sanna, you said,
what goes through your mind at times like this?

Soon at Rudh Dubh, by the slabby stones,
your watercolour really captures it.

Then a boggy patch through birch and heather,
we lost our way and found it again.

Up a crease in the hill, up skittery schist,
we stopped for a moment to catch our breath.

Along grassy paths, past stunted willow,
the roofs of Sanna weren't far below.

Soon we were on to sheep-cropped machair,
the air belonged to cuckoos and skylarks.

Through crushed-shell sand, through bits of kelp,
I felt for the little plover protecting its nest.

The sea was choppy, dark blue, turquoise,
a fishing boat hauled in its catch of crabs.

Tucked into damp clefts of gabbro rock,
sedges, ferns, thrift and wild orchids.

And as skylark choruses drifted across
the bones of abandoned houses, like airborne elegies,

we could only guess why people had once come here,
along the sea-roads and peaty tracks.

Or as they still come, wending over the hills from Kilchoan
Where they now perch, solid in their jaunty new-builds.

Time to turn back, empty boots of singing sand,
hang on to the sea-shrift, sound-drift of Sanna as long
as we can.

Black Wing Rock

That day on the shore at Gullane,
a thousand scoters,
were congregating on the Forth,
an elongating crease of feather and bone
moving as one in the milky sea,
rising forwards, drifting down,
thronging, mobbing,
as the hills of Fife went from gold
to black and we sat on the square rock,
the dog nesting in the sand,
watching the folding and unfolding of wings,
looking back, past the islands, the pilot boats,
the waiting tankers, as if seeing it all
for the first time.

A Dead Lamb in Polbain

How long the lamb had lived,
how long its fleece sodden by the rain,
lent covering for its body lying by the wall,

while other sheep and lambs
ranged over the steep hillside
opposite Tanera Mor,

only its mother knew.
And as she moved away to feed,
the farmer in his boiler suit,

stepped over a low stone wall
and kneeling beside the lamb,
tied its back legs together with twine.

As the lifeless animal was pulled gently
over stones, grass and reeds,
its mother followed in slow procession

across the fields, the lamb's only chance
to be with the flock.
When I next caught sight of the farmer,

the lamb was gone,
its body to the sea-gods, the crow-gods,
its skin to clothe a foundling.

Doggerland

Not the horned beast drowned and rotting in the swamp
the trembling of hooves through my bones
or water seeping through the earth as I sleep
makes the stink of fear
it's the sea-fowl   tree-dwellers   ground-creepers
moving like I've never seen them before
un-settling   un-nesting
skittering through the air as if anything they light on
might kill them
along the hills and ridges   across the tops of trees
all seeking higher land
never resting
all of them fleeing
the winged   the furred   the tusked   the hooved
the small   the tall   the weak   the dangerous
the gods are tormenting them
and us   we're all leaving too
we don't know where
if we don't go soon
we'll be overtaken
hunters from far away say
the white mountains are melting
river tongues are bleeding out
look   water is rising all around us
where will we go when fires are damp
beasts have fled
while there's still soil to tread and animals ahead of me
I'll sharpen my spear and throw it
no matter if it misses   breaks   or is lost forever in the
circling sea

8–10,000 years ago Britain was connected to Europe and Scandinavia by an ancient land mass, now known as Doggerland, long inhabited before being completely submerged by what is now the North Sea, as a result of melting glaciers and a tsunami.

Earth's Witnesses

That time he picked up an inconspicuous stone
from Cromarty beach and hit it with his hammer,
did he imagine a sculptor would one day,
chisel out the moment, his hair and beard,
his coat and trousers from a marble block?

How she'd got the gist of him observing his left hand
cupped around a fossil fish, the plaid folded
across his shoulder, his left leg bent, sunlight sifting
through the Museum cupola, seven centuries and seven
statues away from an Indian Buddha, one of them
in burnished stone the other translucent marble,
both deity and man transfixed in wonder.

Statue of Hugh Miller 'The Witness' by Amelia Paton Hill, Edinburgh 1860s.
Buddha from Bihar, India, 12th Century in Earth Witness pose.
National Museum of Scotland.

The Deskford Carnyx

Hear that?

Sucked out of the dark bog, a sound
once beaten out of fire and battle-blood,
has risen up through thousands of years,
encased in a broken bronze boar's head,
eye-less, tongue-less, with upturned snout.
Once these instruments of war were carried
proud and high on brazen tubes, they filled
the air with their noise, stirring the souls
of warriors, poets, summoned by the gods,
chilling the hearts of foes. Now they're all
forgotten, buried and the trumpet-voice
is the last witness from the past to open
its mouth.

A carnyx or Iron Age trumpet was found in north-east Scotland
around 1816

Sennacherib's Sculptor and the Winged Bulls

'Carve me spirits to guard the gates at Nineveh,
sculpt me Lamassu like the ones at Nimrud.
Make it an impenetrable fortress, a citadel,
a *palace without rival,*' said Sennacherib,
the Assyrian king.

I told him I'd seen the famous winged bulls and lions,
with their human faces, beards, hats and braided hair.
All Assyria was in awe of their size and power.
If only the king had allowed me to get on with the job
without mithering in my ear.
He insisted on meddling in everything.
He was there at the quarry, supervising transport,
presiding over every aspect of my work.
Only in the cool mornings, when kites and cranes
overflew the desert, did I get any time to contemplate
the marks I'd made and the spirits emerging from the
stone.

And at those times, as the heat of the morning grew,
I'd console myself thinking, well at least,
once I've long gone, these winged creatures
will be here at the gates of Nineveh, until the stars
stop shining and the sky falls in.

The Lamassu, or winged bulls and lions, were carved in the 11th-8th
centuries BCE.
36

Bridge

A bridge is an audacious thing,
it challenges the status quo,
it says fling a rope,
throw up some pillars
across a river, ravine, railway track;
hold someone's hand,
don't look down,
hang on to an arm,
hold on until smoke blows up in your face,
don't let go;
shout hello from a bridge too far,
a bridge to nowhere,
a bridge in the desert.
Take Tello,
halfway between Basra and Baghdad,
where the oldest bridge in the world is being rebuilt,
by refugee women and the British Museum.
A bridge to bridge
the centuries,
from terrorism to tourism,
mud-fired brick is being placed on to mud-fired brick,
as step by step,
minds turn away from war,
and part of ancient Iraq is restored.

A team of archaeologists from the British Museum trained teams of refugee
women in Iraq in the conservation of ancient sites, based at the oldest bridge
in the world in Tello, Iraq.

La Mer de Glace

Turn still cold year.
At four in the morning
there's a chill human fug.
Outside the air is thin.
The sun strips back the black
from a massif choked with old snow.
Azure crystals thicken the sky
and the mountains are
close enough to touch.

Boot-deep tracks
file downhill to
la Mer de Glace.
Ice punches through ice
exposing the earth's broken bones.
Crevasses open
and close again, silent tombs.

Glacial streams run off
cliffs of dirty ice, aeons high.
Look back:
A white sea has darkened to rubble,
the glacier has thrown up its bodies
and all the mountains are naked of snow.

Photographed by John Ruskin in 1854, and Emma Stibbon in 2018

Twenty-one Antler Head-dresses, Star Carr

In the time it took
to hear a raven croak
I saw their heads
each rammed with a charred deer skull,
whole branches, halved antlers, broken tips –
moving as one,
silent as a ghost moon,
through birch trees beside a quiet lake,
stalking something.

After that shout, the rush,
feet crushing thick undergrowth
and the bellows of a dying animal.

They're still here, beyond sound,
chanting voices, reverent voices,
out-breaths, smouldering out the brains of deer,
long buried in the peat.

The Death of Echo

I thought we were on the cusp of love
shush shush
some days we seemed to be going places
but for all he cared I could have been a bird
clearing my throat
cough cough
I could have said the first thing that came into my head
like stop playing games with me mister Narcissus
narcosis narcosis
then he tricked me into saying I loved him
that self-obsessed con-artist
was only interested in his own reflection
shun shun
he stole my thoughts
now I'm dying for love
of a chimera
thief thief
I'm a ghost of myself
lost lost
he became a swank of jonquils
a wafting poesie of affodyles
daffodils daffodils
besotted with themselves
whereas I haunt every mountain and empty room
I'm a lament stuck on repeat
grief grief
a refrain caught inside hollow trees
quiet as the whirring wings of bumblebees
hum hum

Shoe Doll in the City Arts Centre, Edinburgh

So many faces peer at me through the ages, through the
glass –
a bearded grimace scratched on to a medieval piss-pot,
those *whit ya nebbin' a* glares from Bellany's fish-gutters,
but the face that draws me back consists of two triangles
of paper for eyes, another for a mouth, a strip for a nose,
all glued to the heel of a shoe.

A girl on a doorstep in London ignored everyone
around her as she unwrapped a parcel. A flat face
stared out surrounded by bootnails and behind the face,
black material edged with a frill was fashioned into a
bonnet.
Then she saw the scarf, apron and dress tied around its
body.
Was it once a thrill for her to cradle, to include in games,
to talk to, to sit at a table? I wonder who, with so little,
gave a worn shoe a new purpose, a child so much love?

Shoe Doll originally found in London.

Washerwomen on Calton Hill

Scunnered. Such a good day
for drying clothes up on the hill, away
from all the smoky lums and up he comes,
wants us to pose on the slopes.
The cheek of him, we were all in position,
standing, kneeling and his box on legs all set up,
when he asked us to wait while he runs down to the gorse
to relieve himself!
Eventually he flitted and was gone.
Then one day when I was rushing down Leith Street,
I noticed a picture in the studio window.
I was taken aback by my dark shawl blurred by the breeze,
all the clothes laid on the grass, our white bonnets, long dark dresses,
the bairns' tresses and how that Thomas Begbie had made us look
like ourselves but more elegant and had squeezed us all
out of his box on to one small square of paper.

Washerwomen on Calton Hill, Edinburgh, calotype by Thomas Begbie, 1887

What'cha

I could have
missed that look
from a pillar of glass
indifferent as a lighthouse
aloof as a distant megalith.
Another day
I might have passed you by
instead you made me curious
as you looked out
with outstretched hands,
stark with silica, shells
and perforations. Who
were you watching and why?
Was your opaqueness
malign or divine?
A man with a walking frame
paused beside me, kept
asking my name
and when I glanced back
your gaze had moved on,
you were unreachable,
gone.

Inspired by Watcher III Bertil Vallien. Glass, sand cast.
Kostas, Sweden 2006. National Museum of Scotland.

Frosty Leo

Through the glass, a cloud of ice grains
was spilling through the ether, obscuring
an exploding star. It was collapsing
into its own core, defying its own demise,
becoming brighter than ever, becoming
a supernova, an expanding mass, exploding
in an ice storm, hundreds of miles above the earth.
On board the Stratospheric Observatory,
an astronomer noted, IRAS 09371+1212,
dying star Frosty in Leo galaxy, emitting blips
of light every 200 seconds, is being swallowed
by a black hole.
As an afterthought he scribbled,
Is it fanciful to think this star might be screaming?

Andromeda on All Hallows' Eve

Leaving the light of the caravan,
I was half expecting the creels
emptying out the crows and jackdaws,
the tidal fields of gulls and geese,
pyres of buckthorn, hawthorn, rowan,
waves of storm-lobbed clouds
but when night bolted the door
I saw stars unravel,
constellations snap into place.
Then east of Cassiopeia
a tight-knit galaxy, a luminous coven,
concealed in a cloak of its own brilliance,
moving through the thin end of the year,
almost silent.

Goodbye Voyager 1

I heard you made it
to interstellar space
past the kiss-me-quick hats
lost balloons
stratus and noctilucent clouds
satellites and meteorites
the ever-orbiting bits of junk like me
Telstar 1963
all the way through the heliosphere
beyond the outer planets
if only I could have been programmed
to be as brave as you
do you remember you played
Stravinsky and Chuck Berry
when we almost collided all those years ago
now look where your heart's desire
has got you to
travelling on a one-way ticket
through thickets of universes
black holes and dying stars
to immortality
where you belong
over and out
so long

ABOUT ARACHNE PRESS

Arachne Press is a micro publisher of (award-winning!) short story and poetry anthologies and collections, novels including a Carnegie Medal nominated young adult novel, and a photographic portrait collection.

We are expanding our range all the time, but the short form is our first love. We keep fiction and poetry live, through readings, festivals (in particular our Solstice Shorts Festival), workshops, exhibitions and all things to do with writing.

Follow us on Twitter:
@ArachnePress
@SolShorts

Like us on Facebook:
ArachnePress
SolsticeShorts2014

Recent poetry from Arachne Press

In Retail Jeremy Dixon
ISBN: 978-1-909208-72-8 £8.99
While working in a well-known pharmacy chain, Jeremy Dixon found surprising inspiration. His poems were written on the ends of till rolls and smuggled out in his socks.
Anyone who has ever worked in retail will recognise the characters and situations, and the management-speak absurdities; but Jeremy also brings his perspective as a queer writer to bear, with witty and wicked results.

The Knotsman Math Jones
ISBN: 978-1-909208-73-5 £9.99
The Knotsman does not exist, you will not find him in history books or collections of 'bygone' skills. But Math Jones has created him, and his fellows, in a time very like the English Civil War.
There he is, going from house to house, village to village, poem to poem, battlefield to gallows, unravelling knots and problems, physical, emotional and psychological; a new kind of cunning man, not always welcome, not always quite as clever as his fingers and picks would have him believe.

Mamiaith Ness Owen
ISBN: 978-1-909208-77-3 £8.99
Ness Owen lives on Ynys Môn off the North Wales coast. This is her first collection, and is partly bilingual. The poems journey widely from family and motherhood, to politics, place and belonging: an underlying connection to the earth of Ness's home, that feeds a longing/desire/determination to write in the Mamiaith (mother tongue) that she speaks, but did not learn to write fluently. The interplay of languages and the shifts of meaning from one to the other feed the musicality of the poems.